WARBIRDS ILLUSTRATED No 41

Cover illustration: A new Lockheed Vega-built B-17G on a test flight over southern California in mid-1943. (Lockheed-California)

1. A new arrival to the European Theatre of Operations (ETO) during a practice mission with the 91st BG, 28 January 1944. The B-17G was Boeing's final version of the Flying Fortress. (USAF)

B-17 FLYING FORTRESS

JEFFREY ETHELL

ARMS AND ARMOUR PRESS

Introduction

Published in 1986 by Arms & Armour Press Ltd., 2–6 Hampstead High Street, London NW3 1QQ.

Distributed in the United States by Sterling Publishing Co. Inc., 2 Park Avenue, New York, N.Y. 10016.

© Arms & Armour Press Ltd., 1986
All rights reserved. No part of this publication may be reproduced, stored in a retrieval system, or transmitted in any form by any means electrical, mechanical or otherwise, without first seeking the written permission of the copyright owner.

British Library Cataloguing in Publication Data:
Ethell, Jeffrey
B-17 Flying Fortress. – (Warbirds illustrated; no. 41)
1. B-17 bomber
I. Title II. Series
623.74'63   UG1242.B6

ISBN 0-85368-767-6

Editing, design and artwork by Roger Chesneau. Typesetting by Typesetters (Birmingham) Ltd. Printed and bound in Italy by GEA/GEP in association with Keats European Ltd., London.

◄2
2. Flying Fortresses sometimes got in each other's way. Over Berlin on 19 May 1944 500-pounders from one 94th BG B-17 knocked the left horizontal stabilizer and elevator off another aircraft below. Even though the stricken B-17F flew straight and level until it crashed, no one got out. (USAF)

The Boeing Aircraft Company's B-17 Flying Fortress is, without much doubt, America's most famous military aircraft. Considered to be one of the major weapons of the Second World War, this four-engined bomber was held in very high esteem by Army Air Forces leaders: after the war, for example, General Carl 'Tooey' Spaatz told AAF chief General Hap Arnold that 'the B-17 was the single weapon most responsible for the defeat of Germany'.

Ordered by the US Army Air Corps in August 1934, the Model 299 flew for the first time on 28 July 1935 but was not designated B-17 until the following January. The aircraft was tested at Wright Field in fly-offs against the Martin 146 (an improved B-10) and the Douglas DB-1 (based on the DC-2 and later designated B-18). Without question the 250mph Boeing, carrying eight 600lb bombs, was far superior to the competition, but when the prototype Model 299 crashed because its controls were inadvertently locked on take-off the B-18 won the Air Corps contract. Boeing was brought to the brink of financial disaster, with the loss of over $6 million, but an Army order for thirteen test Y1B-17s kept the programme – and the company – alive. The next major development, the Y1B-17A, incorporated turbo-superchargers, giving excellent high-altitude performance. There was a hint that the Air Corps dream of a long-range strategic bombardment capability might be fulfilled, but the aircraft was not presented in this way.

The B-17 was sold to Congress as the ultimate 'defensive' weapon, reflecting the spirit of the isolationist prewar years: the bomber would be flown to protect US shores and overseas possessions from enemy fleets – in other words, this marvel of engineering would be an extended form of coastal artillery. However, within the Air Corps a determined cadre of believers in the B-17 began to manoeuvre behind the scenes to get the superior aircraft ordered in quantity. In February and March 1938, within a year of their delivery, Y1B-17s attached to the 2nd Bomb Group made two goodwill flights to South America. Numerous records were broken, leading to a headline campaign to convince Congress and the public that the B-17 was worth having, and from that point on the Flying Fortress began to take its place in history. From one Y1B-17 built every two weeks in 1937, Fortress production jumped to a peak of sixteen per day in April 1944; by the time it was all over, 12,731 B-17s had been built.

This book, compiled with the help of the many individuals and organizations named in the photo credits, should give some idea of just how versatile an aircraft the B-17 was. A special word of thanks goes to Larry Webb who spent his holidays in the darkroom to print most of the shots included here.

Jeffrey L. Ethell

▲3

3. Although the XB-15 did not fly until 26 months after the Model 299, it served, along with the Boeing 247, as a design basis for that aircraft, which was later designated B-17. Only a single XB-15 was built. (USAF)

4. X13372, the prototype Boeing 299, in 1935. Despite its destruction during competition flights against the Martin B-10 and Douglas B-18, the successful aircraft paved the way for the Flying Fortress series. (G. S. Williams via Roger F. Besecker)

5. Seen here at Wright Field in 1936, 36-149 was one of thirteen service test Y1B-17s. Hanging on by a thread through skimpy Congressional funding, the B-17 programme was sold as a 'defensive' weapon. (Roger F. Besecker)

6. A Y1B-17 of the 96th BS, 2nd BG, during operational evaluation of the aircraft in the late 1930s. (Roger Freeman)

▼4

7. The six Y1B-17s of the 49th BS, 2nd BG, which made the February 1938 South American Goodwill Flight, seen here over New York. (Roger Freeman)

8. The sleek lines of this 2nd BG Y1B-17 heralded the dawn of a new age for the US Army Air Corps, which would become a separate service in under ten years.

9. The 38th Reconnaissance Squadron was one of the few units which managed to operate its Y1B-17s in other than the strategic bombardment role.

10. A 2nd BG Y1B-17 at Hillsgrove, Rhode Island, 20 April 1939. (Harlie Wood via Norm Taylor)

9▲ 10▼

▲11
11. The B-17B incorporated a number of improvements, including turbo-superchargers, a larger rudder, changes to the fuel system and a redesigned nose. An aircraft commander's 'bubble' was added to the top of the rear cockpit area. (Norm Taylor)
12. The next generation B-17C was sold to the RAF as the Fortress Mk I. No. 90 Squadron introduced the aircraft to combat over Europe, but it was badly mauled by Luftwaffe fighters. This example is seen over England on 2 August 1941. (Roger Freeman)
13. The first significant American use of the 'Fort' in combat was with the 5th Air Force out of New Guinea in 1942. Here two B-17Es of the 43rd BG sit at Port Moresby as a DC-5 takes off. (Frank F. Smith)
14. A 5th AF B-17E sits in a revetment at Port Moresby, New Guinea, 1 November 1942. (USAF)

▼12

13▲ 14▼

▲15

▲16 ▼17

15. P-39s take off over 'Tojo's Jinx', a B-17E of the 19th BG, at Port Moresby, New Guinea, on 19 August 1942. The starboard side of the nose carried the name 'Frank Buck'. (Frank F. Smith)

16, 17. The same B-17 as that shown in the previous photograph, after it force-landed on a New Guinea beach a few months later near Port Moresby. Natives helped to lay down enough steel matting to enable the bomber to take off and make it back to base. (Frank F. Smith)

18. Jackson's Drome, Port Moresby: 'Talisman', a B-17F, taxis out for a mission on 5 September 1943. General Douglas MacArthur flew in this aircraft to view New Guinea battle zones. (USAF)

19. 'Sally' was 5th AF commander Maj-Gen. George C. Kenney's personal B-17E. Declared war weary with the arrival of new -F models, and stripped of all paint and left with only the top turret, she made quite a transport! (USAF)

20. In November 1943 this B-17E was converted into 'Bataan', an XC-108 which served as General MacArthur's personal transport. It had 'airliner' portholes, a tail turret position modified for better vision, and no paint. Here it sits at Fairbairn, Canberra, Australia, on 18 March 1944. (Frank F. Smith)

18▲ 19▲ 20▼

▲21 ▼22

21. MacArthur's 'Bataan' in New Caledonia. The 'plushed-out' -E model had a galley in what used to be the radio room, reclining seats in the waist area, reading lights and even hot and cold running water. (USAF)
22. After Operation 'Torch', the Allied invasion of North Africa in November 1942, B-17s were transferred from England and living conditions changed drastically: the 97th BG's base at Biskra often appeared to be idyllic, but living in the desert and fighting a war was a nightmare. North African mud was merciless to both sides. This B-17F sank into the ground taxying across the desert turf. (VMI)
23. The B-17's nose was an ideal 'canvas' for art, as can be seen on this B-17F under repair. (USAF)
24. A 97th BG B-17F returns to its base at Biskra, North Africa, with one propeller feathered, 31 December 1942. (VMI)

▲25 ▼26

25. As the war got under way numerous patrols were flown from Panama in expectation of an attack on the Canal. The hours and hours of over-water flying meant extremely boring duty for crews supposedly on combat status. (USAF)

26. Seemingly at the other end of the world, a B-17F attached to the 2nd Service Group warms up at Meeks Field, Iceland, 23 April 1943. The bone-chilling cold could never be kept out of the draughty 'Forts'. (USAF)

27. From February 1943 until salvage in December 1944, B-17F 'Meat Hound' faithfully served the 423rd BS, 306th BG. The 8th Air Force began combat operations in August 1942 against some of the best defences in the world. (USAF)

28. Many aircraft brought down over enemy territory proved to be suitable for repair and evaluation. This captured B-17E sits at Orly, Paris, in December 1942, ready for transfer to what would later become *Zirkus Rosarias*, the Luftwaffe enemy equipment unit. (Roger F. Besecker)

▲29

▲30 ▼31

29. ATA pilots and their friends await the arrival of two 91st BG 'Forts' as an RAF Hurricane and Fairchild stand by. (Merle Olmsted)
30. A 325th BS, 92nd BG B-17G stands ready for its 11th mission, England, 1943. (Ed Lile via Norm Taylor)
31. 'Just-A-Snappin', of the 418th BS, leads the 13th Combat Bomb Wing to Regensburg during the North African Shuttle mission of 17 August 1943. The pilot was Capt. Evert Blakeley with group ops officer Maj. John B. Kidd serving as co-pilot. (John Kidd via Ian Hawkins)
32. Just below 'Virgin's Delight', a Messerschmitt Bf 109 is seen 'split-essing' for earth after making an attack run on the 91st BG as the bombers were on their way to Emden, 27 September 1943. (USAF)
33. 'Somewhere over France', a 'Fort' breaks up and goes down before reaching the target. (USAF)

▲34 ▼35

34. 'Hell's Angels', of the 303rd BG, became one of the more famous of the early B-17Fs to see combat. Here parked at Molesworth on 10 October 1943, she bears testimony to the trips she has taken into Fortress Europe. The 303rd as a unit would later adopt her name. (USAF)

35. On the way back from Bremen on 8 October 1943, 'Just-A-Snappin' crash-landed at Ludham, Norfolk; No. 4 propeller, which had windmilled since being hit over the target, fell off on the landing roll. Someone counted over 800 holes from the radio room back. (John Kidd via Ian Hawkins)

36. Radar was introduced for bombing through overcasts, and here a 351st BG PFF lead-ship lines up on German ports on 13 December 1943. Fifteen other B-17s can be counted above the clouds. (USAF)

36

37. A 390th BG 'Fort' bores in from the IP towards the Me 110 plant at Waggum. (USAF)

38. After AAF formations got so heavily mauled by German fighters, the YB-40, a gunship designed to fly in the middle of formations, was developed, but it proved to be so heavy – and it rarely got any more hits than other 'Forts' – that it was withdrawn from service. These YB-40s are seen at Bassingbourne during their combat trials. (Marion Havelaar via Merle Olmsted)

39. 94th BG 'Forts' return from the target on 26 September 1943 still with their external 1,000lb bombs after finding the ground obscured by cloud. The additional drag and weight reduced range and altitude so drastically that this modification was used only on special occasions. (USAF)

40. When bombing on PFF (radar), a smoke marker had to be used to guide the formations in. In this photograph the smoke trail can be seen running under the noses of the two lead-ships on the way to Bremen. (USAF)

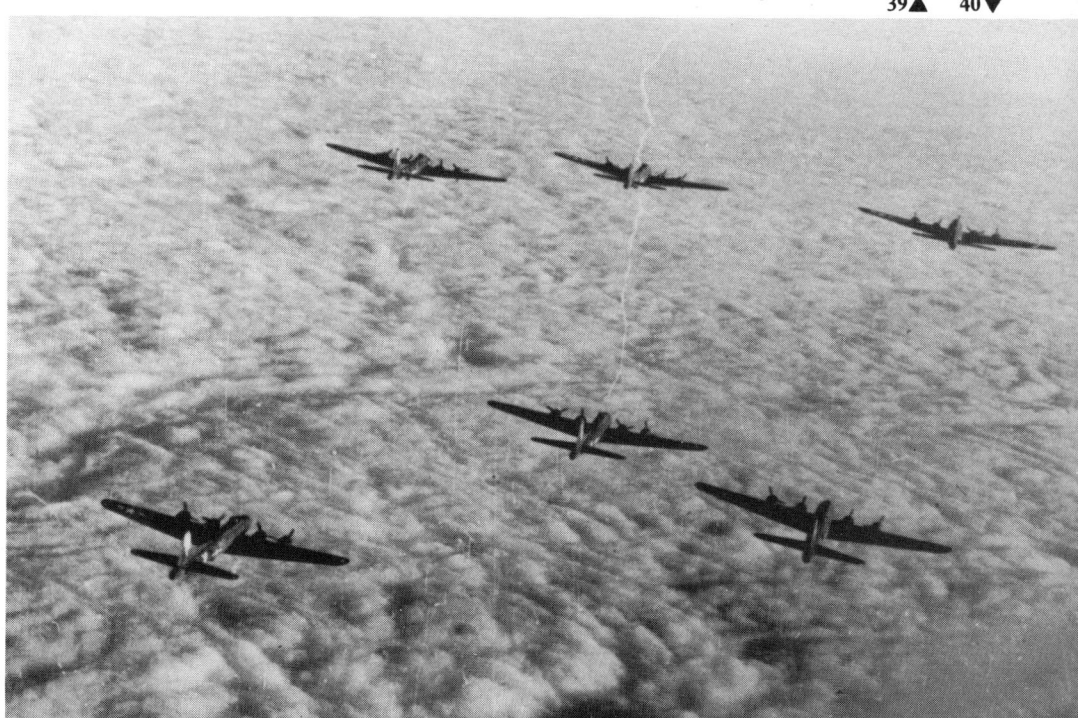

▲41

41. The 401st BG on the way back from Ludwigshaven. (USAF)
42. A 401st BG B-17G on finals at Deenthorpe. (Roger Freeman)
43. A B-17C attached to Wright Field's Material Division undergoes service testing. Though the name 'Flying Fortress' had been popular since the aircraft's roll-out, it would be some time before the aircraft was fitted with extensive defensive armament. (NASM)
44. A brand new B-17F, along with its companions, awaits assignment to a USAAF unit. (USAF)

▼42

43▲ 44▼

▲45

45. A ZI- (Zone of the Interior) based training B-17 takes on fuel in the south-east United States. (NASM)

46. 91st Bomb Group Flying Fortresses try to find a hole to hit the airfield at Meulan les Mureaux, France, where the Dornier assembly plant was located, 3 September 1943. (USAF)

47. 'Five Grand' was the 5,000th B-17 built at Seattle after Pearl Harbor. Every worker involved managed to sign her, and she went to war with the 96th Bomb Group, 8th Air Force, flying 78 missions. (USAF)

48. Though a study in marked contrasts, this B-17G and Piper L-4 Cub (photographed in England during the Second World War) were not that different, according to 'Fort' pilots. The most common accolade on how easy the B-17 was to fly was that it landed 'just like a great big Cub'. (USAF)

▼46

47 ▲   48 ▼

49. Major James McPartlin, pilot of the 91st Bomb Group's 'General Ike' in England, gets a dunking at Bassingbourne after flying his first mission. (USAF)

50–52. The A-2 leather jackets worn by USAAF crews often duplicated the nose art of their aircraft, though at the cost of few bottles of choice bourbon if the whole crew got the treatment! These three photographs represent some of the aircraft flown by the 401st BG out of England. (USAF)

◀49

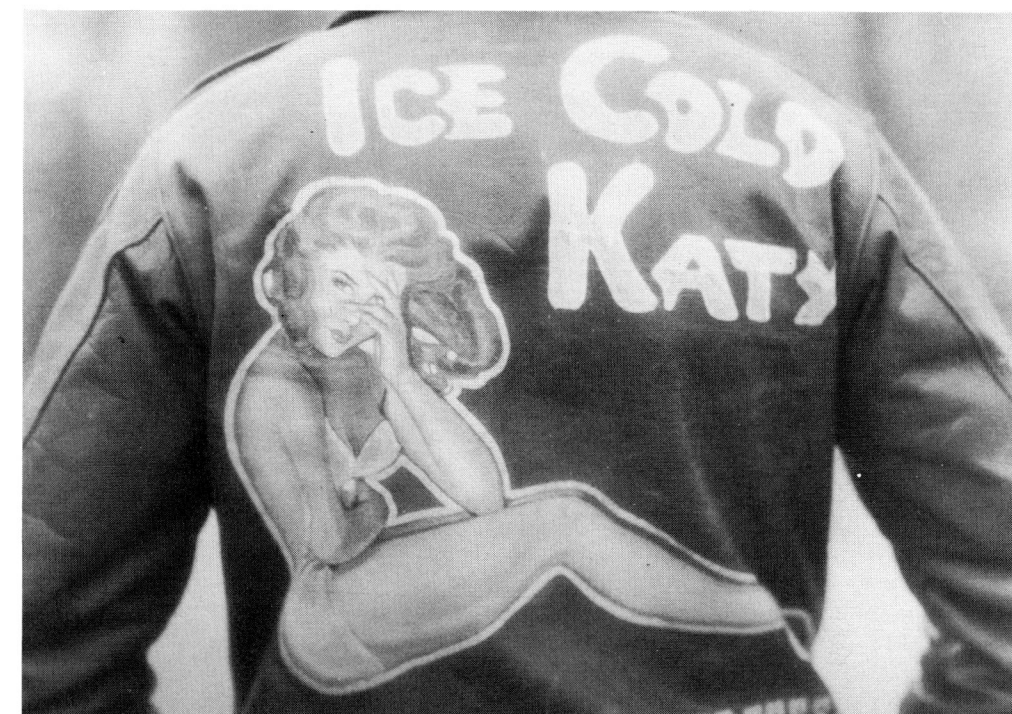

50▲ 51▼ 52▼

▲53

53. A B-17 of the 401st BG takes on 2,700 gallons of fuel, before flying a raid against Oranienburg, 10 March 1944. (USAF)
54. The 91st BG on the way to Oberpfaffenhofen, 18 March 1944. (USAF)
55. On 1 November 1944 the 379th BG's 'Swamp Fire' became the first 8th AF 'heavy' to complete 100 missions without a mechanical abort. After take-off the No. 2 engine failed, but the group CO radioed to 'proceed to target even if you lose all engines – I want that record!' The aircraft bombed an alternative target in France and came home, and by the time 'Swamp Fire' was finally brought down over Belgium she had flown 120 missions. Here crew chief M/Sgt De Salvo paints on the hundredth symbol. (Bill Smith via Merle Olmsted)
56. 2nd Lt. Homer Glass and Sgt. Robert Megchelsen look over their flak-punctured tail tyre which was hit over Berlin. (USAF)

▼54

55 ▲ 56 ▼

31

57. A 379th BG 'Fort' settles on its tail while making a belly-landing in England. Note that the radio room hatch has already been pulled inside for quick egress. (Bill Smith via Merle Olmsted)

58. Flak just about took the nose off this 379th BG 'Fort', but it made it back home with a fierce wind shrieking back through the fuselage. (Bill Smith via Merle Olmsted)

59. The 401st BG's 'Boche Buster', with a good-sized hole through her vertical stabilizer, limped to Sweden on 7 October 1944. She was an original group ship, having been delivered on 19 November 1943. (Bert Hocking via Merle Olmsted)

60. Fortresses under fire: the 303rd BG releases its load on Wiesbaden at 1054hrs on 15 August 1944.

59▲ 60▼

33

▲61 ▼62

34

61. On 15 October 1944 this 91st BG took a flak hit in the waist and ball turret. (USAAF via Norm Taylor)
62. 'Old Ironsides' (IW-X) and 'Chute the Works' (IW-F) make up part of the 401st BG on the way into Germany in late 1944. (Ralph Trout via Merle Olmsted)
63. In place of the ball turret many lead-ships, like this one from the 401st BG, began to carry a radar scanner during the last year of the war. Numerous missions were flown using radar, although the results were quite poor. (Ralph Trout via Merle Olmsted)
64. Smoke markers winding down, a 'Fort' passes over the target.

65. Shiny natural metal B-17Gs of the 452nd BG head out over an overcast towards Germany in early 1945. Crews were initially fearful that the lack of camouflage paint would make their aircraft easy targets, but the weight savings and no increase in losses showed the move to be wise.

66–70. Late 1944 and early 1945 saw the 8th Air Force reign supreme over what was left of Hitler's empire. The gleaming 'Forts' took their place in history, giving the 'Queen of the Sky' undisputed fame. These B-17Gs of the 306th, 384th, 381st and 91st BGs are on their way to make adjustments to the 'Thousand Year Reich'. (USAF)

▲65

▲66 ▼67

68▲

69▲ 70▼

▲71

71. 'Wicked Witch' was assigned to the 91st BG for its combat tour. The nose decor was painted by the group's top artist, Tony Starcer, who was responsible for the famous renderings on 'Memphis Belle', 'Shoo, Shoo, Shoo Baby' and many more. (William Cornell via Norm Taylor)
72. After being shot up over Germany, this 324th BS, 91st BG B-17G belly-landed at Bassingbourne. (William Cornell via Norm Taylor)
73, 74. One of the 100th BG's radar ships – witness the scanner in place of the ball turret. (Chris Goodman via Norm Taylor)

▼72

73 ▲ 74 ▼

75. The 91st BG delivers its load on Berlin, 28 February 1945. (USAF)
76. Flying at 25,500ft, lead aircraft of the 389th BG approach the Huls August benzol plant, 8 March 1945. (Barney Lucas)
77. The high squadron of the 398th BG on the way to the Ulm marshalling yards at 23,000ft over a very thick undercast, 4 March 1945. (Barney Lucas)
78. Lead-ships of the 398th BG stretch out at 22,300ft over the Dillenburg marshalling yards, bombing by PFF, 12 March 1945. (Barney Lucas)
79. (Next spread) At 23,500ft, the 303rd BG begins its run on the Zossen Army HQ near Berlin, 15 March 1945. (Barney Lucas)

▲80

80. Near the Oranienburg marshalling yards, the 398th BG begins its run at 23,000ft, 15 March 1945. (Barney Lucas)
81. A 351st BG radar-ship, with scanner and bomb doors extended, prepares to drop its bombs over Germany. (Barney Lucas)
82. On 6 July 1944, 18-year-old Princess Elizabeth christened her namesake, 'Rose of York', at Thurleigh, England. The aircraft was originally to have been named 'Princess Elizabeth', but the inevitable German propaganda that would have resulted were the B-17 to go down caused a change of mind. (USAF)

▼81 82▶

▲83 ▼84

83. 'Suzy-Q' was one of the veteran B-17Es of the early Pacific War. Leaving Seattle on 1 January 1942, she made her way east across the United States and on to Java. She flew numerous missions, then retreated to Australia to fight in the Battle of the Coral Sea and over New Guinea, Rabaul, Truk and several other Japanese strongholds, until coming back to San Francisco on 1 January 1943, having circumnavigated the globe. (USAF)
84. No Second World War B-17 unit could keep all its aircraft in hangars, and most of the maintenance was done out in the open, come rain or snow, so that aircraft could be kept operational. (USAF)
85. The 91st Bomb Group on the way to France in May 1943, led by 'Mary Ruth – Memories of Mobile'. (USAF)
86. One lesson to which every crew paid attention – how to ditch the B-17. Due to its flush lower wing, the 'Fort' had excellent ditching and belly-landing characteristics, which meant a high probability of survival. (USAF)

▲87 ▼88

87. Long after its combat days were over, the B-17 was cast in a number of secondary roles. This VB-17G, sitting at Taegu (K-2), was a VIP transport attached to HQ FEAF (Far East Air Forces) during the Korean War. (David McLaren)

88. The US Coast Guard used PB-1s (B-17Gs) for search and rescue well into the late 1950s. This one sits at Logan Field in Boston, May 1955. (P. Paulsen via Dave Menard)

89. Berlin was a target that the 8th Air Force and the RAF continued to hit hard for the last year of the war. Here the 390th BG nears the IP on 18 March 1945 at 26,000ft. (Barney Lucas)

90. The low squadron of the 398th BG nears the Derben oil dump at 19,250ft, 8 April 1945. (Barney Lucas)

▲91

▲92 ▼93

91. With only a few clouds in the background, the yellow-tailed 447th BG is seen on the way to Kiel's U-boat pens, 3 April 1945. (Barney Lucas)

92. Contrails were a curse and blessing: they helped enemy fighters and flak, but also friendly aircraft, trying to find the bomber stream. Here the lead-ship in the 398th BG low squadron navigates towards Chemnitz at 28,600ft on 5 March 1945. (Barney Lucas)

93. The low squadron of the 384th BG ploughs through to the marshalling yards at Schwerte, 10 March 1945. The undercast forced all aircraft to bomb using PFF. (Barney Lucas)

94. Close to fifty Flying Fortresses of the 457th BG head for Chemnitz in March 1945, again using radar (as evidenced by the scanner on the closest ship). (Barney Lucas)

95. As the 398th BG headed for Kohlenbissen airfield on 7 April 1945, *Sonderkommando Elbe*, the Luftwaffe unit created to ram enemy bombers, flew its only known operation against the 8th Air Force. At least eight B-17s and B-24s are thought to have been lost to ramming aircraft. (Barney Lucas)

94▲ 95▼

▲ 96 ▼ 97

96. The 15th Air Force hit strategic targets while flying from bases in Italy. This 414th BS, 97th BG Fortress is leaving the target at Messina, Sicily, 8 May 1943. (USAF)
97. Framed from the waist of another B-17, a 301st BG 'Fort' is seen en route to hit Viterbo Airdrome, Italy, 29 July 1943. (USAF)
98. Tail markings for the 301st BG later changed to a squared 'Y', while '3' stood for the 353rd BS. The rugged Italian Alps had to be crossed every time the 15th Air Force attacked Germany. (USAF)
99. 'Sky Hag' leads a box of 301st BG B-17Fs over Italy. (USAF)

98 ▲   99 ▼

100. Among P-38s, 'Gooney Birds' and Spitfires at Palermo, Sicily, sits a B-17F of the 2nd BG (the first unit to be equipped with Y1B-17s in the late 1930s), 2 October 1943. (USAF)

101. A 96th BS, 2nd BG Flying Fortress being serviced at Foggia, Italy, the 15th AF's major area for basing its bombers and fighters. (Frank F. Smith)

102. A 429th BS, 2nd BG B-17G, having just 'bellied in' at Foggia. Typically, there was no major damage. (Frank F. Smith)

102 ▼

▲103 ▼104

103. 'Forts' taxi out at Celone, Italy (the 463rd BG base), on 6 November 1944. Things were fine until the rain – and the mud – came. (USAF)

104. Taking part in Operation 'Strangle', 348th BS, 99th BG B-17Gs do their best to choke off German supply routes through the centre of Italy. (USAF)

105. The 463rd BG heads out over thickening cloud to attack rail targets in Germany, 3 August 1944. (USAF)

▲106 ▼107

58

106. The 97th BG's B-17G 42-102919 was the first 15th Air Force heavy bomber to land in Russia on the initial Russia Shuttle mission of 2 June 1944. Here a group of Russians and Americans welcome it back from a sortie out of its Ukraine base. (USAF)
107. P-38s weave over the 97th BG as the formation heads for the marshalling yards at Linz, Austria. (USAF)
108. 'Joker' was one of the veteran B-17Gs of the 463rd BG. Note the replacement natural metal tail turret position. (USAF)
109. With a radar equipped 'Fort' leading the way, the 301st BG heads across the Alps for Vienna on 12 March 1945. (USAF)

108▲ 109▼

110. Stablemates: a 451st BG B-24 Liberator leads a crippled 2nd BG B-17G back from Linz, Austria, on 16 March 1945. Shortly after this photograph was taken, the Fortress went down. (USAF)

111. Meanwhile, on the same day, this 419th BS, 301st BG B-17G was heading back for Italy from Floridsdorf, Austria, with its No. 1 propeller feathered. (USAF)

112. With the German surrender in May 1945, bombers were flown back to the United States for ultimate disposal. This 457th BG 'Fort' is being serviced at Bradley Field, Connecticut, following a flight from Europe, 22 May 1945. Many B-24s and B-17s were transferred to the west coast for use in the war with Japan. (Mike Moffitt via Norm Taylor)

113. Although they had been assigned to combat units, many homecoming aircraft, like this 457th B-17G, were in excellent condition, having served only for a short time overseas. (Mike Moffitt via Norm Taylor)

▲110 ▼111

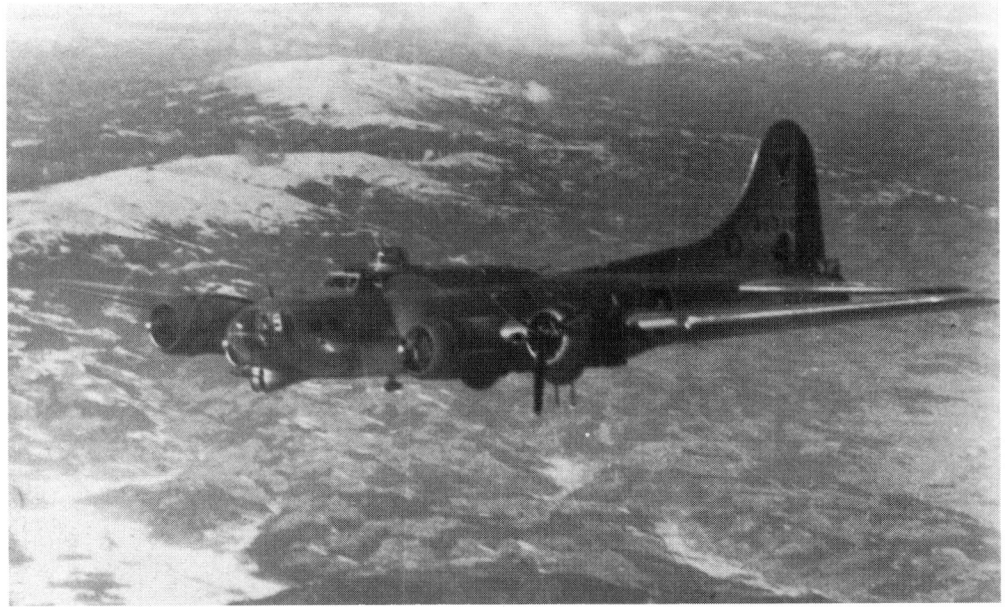

112▲ 113▼

61

▲114 ▼115

114. A B-17G taxis in at Bradley Field in May 1945 after a flight from the 91st BG's base at Bassingbourne, England. (Mike Moffitt via Norm Taylor)

115. Three 'Forts' at Bradley on 22 May 1945, the real veteran being the 457th BG aircraft in the background with a string of mission symbols on the nose and deeply stained engine nacelles. (Mike Moffitt via Norm Taylor)

116, 117. When it became clear that there would be no need for more B-17s in the Pacific, they were put out to pasture all over the United States (but primarily in the dry south-west). With full fuel tanks, hundreds of virtually new 'Forts' are here seen awaiting disposal at Erlangen, Germany, to be either flown home or destroyed on the spot. (USAF via Dave Menard)

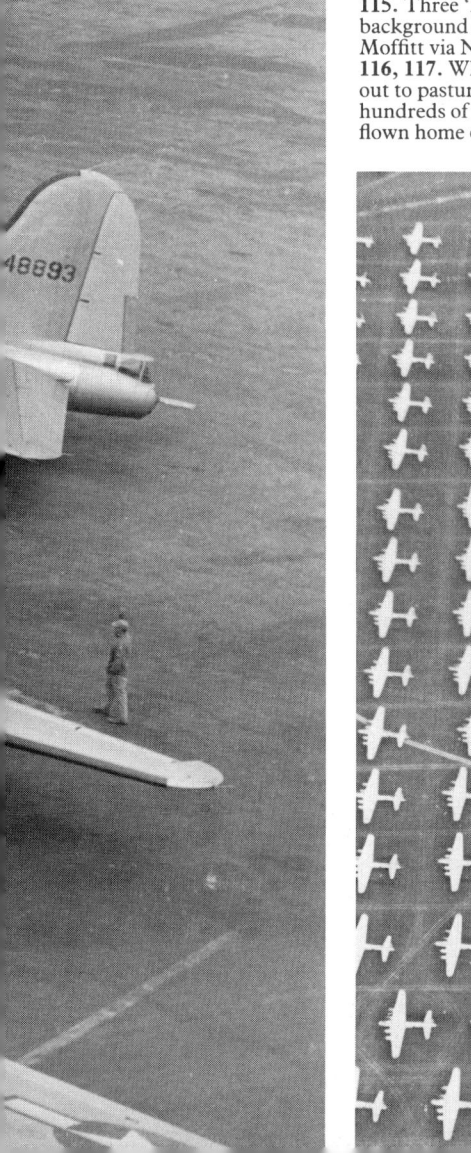

▲118
118. The first air–sea rescue Fortresses went into combat over the Pacific in the last months of the war with full defensive armament, except for the radar scanner in place of the chin turret. A 27ft A-1 lifeboat for aiding fliers brought down over the sea was slung underneath. (Roger F. Besecker)

▼119

119. In April 1946 the USAAF and the US Coast Guard adopted standardized yellow markings for its SB-17s and had all the aircraft stripped of their armament. (Roger F. Besecker via Norm Taylor)

120. A USAF air–sea rescue SB-17 drops its A-1 lifeboat during a service test. (USAF via Dave Menard)

120▲

▲121

▲122 ▼123

121. German V-1 'buzz bombs' were copied in the US as the JB-2 and were mounted on MB-17Gs as air-to-surface missiles. This test flight is being carried out from Wendover, Utah – far away from populated areas. (Merle Olmsted)

122. The All Weather Flying Center at Oakland, California, flew this red-tailed, yellow-chevroned WB-17G in February 1948. The unit became known as the 'Hurricane Hunters', a title passed down with distinction to the present day. (Roger F. Besecker)

123. General Joe Cannon, in common with many other wartime generals, had a B-17G stripped and made into a personal transport, in this case named 'Cannon Ball'. Everyone knew when he was coming. (Roger F. Besecker)

124. Many Flying Fortresses were turned into multi-engine training aircraft, as were B-25s. Here a TB-17G sits at Chanute Air Force Base in 1954. (Merle Olmsted)

125. For Boeing's 30 July 1956 celebration flypast of the company's bombers, the USAF flew one of their remaining operational Flying Fortresses. Though the serial included an 'O' for obsolete, the grand old aircraft was quite a sight with polished skin and white anti-solar fuselage top. (Peter M. Bowers via Dave Menard)

▲126
126. The last USAF 'Forts' were turned into missile targets as QB-17s. This one is seen at Edwards AFB in 1959 in glaring red paint. (Roger F. Besecker)
127. After the Second World War the newly formed USAF turned many B-17s into transports. This B-17G is being refuelled at Rome en route to Iran in July 1949. (Merle Olmsted)
128. This all-black RB-17G, once in the Chinese Nationalist Air Force, was used for clandestine missions in the mid-1950s, dropping agents into South-East Asia. The serial number was 44-
▼127

85531, but the aircraft carried many different numbers on the tail. As can be seen in these photographs (taken at Clark AFB, the Philippines, in September 1957), the ball turret position has been replaced with a door for dropping parachutists. (Merle Olmsted)
129. The fledgling Israeli Air Force flew three B-17Gs in combat during the 1948 War of Independence.
130. Seen here at Miami in June 1959, the ex-US civil B-17G registered N9815F was turned into a freight hauler and finally an insect sprayer for work in South America. (Roger F. Besecker)

128 ▲

129 ▲   130 ▼

▲131 ▼132

131. In order to test its new 5,000hp XT35 turbo-prop engine, the Wright Aeronautical Corporation mounted it to the nose of a Fortress, redesignated EB-17G and finally JB-17G. Here one of Wright's R-3350 Constellation engines is mounted to the aircraft. (Tom Cuddy via Roger F. Besecker)

132. The Wright test-bed eventually became a borate bomber, and is seen here at Black Hills Airport, South Dakota, on 3 June 1967. This aircraft certainly gets the award for ugliest B-17 ever, with blunt nose and non-standard Curtiss electric props. (Norm Taylor)

133. Pratt & Whitney converted another 'Fort' in similar fashion to test its 5,500hp XT34 turbo-prop; note that all four Wright Cyclone piston engines have their propellers feathered. Both the long-nose conversions were designated Model 299Z by Boeing. (Norm Taylor)

▲134

▲135 ▼136

134. This PB-1G, at Travis Field, Georgia, in August 1963, was turned into a crop-duster for Dothan Aviation in Alabama. The company eventually sold all of its aircraft, and only a few are now airworthy. (Hartman via Norm Taylor)

135. This rare B-17F flew as a fire bomber for many years. After the war it was used as a TB-17, then made into an outdoor monument. Following a legal battle, it was sold and made airworthy. When this photograph was taken (at Anchorage, Alaska, on 5 June 1969), the aircraft still carried some of the markings and paint from its appearance in the film *Tora! Tora! Tora!* In 1986 it was being restored by the Seattle Museum of Flight to its former historic glory. Now that the Flying Fortress has become so rare, most of the airworthy examples are being purchased from fire-bombing organizations to be flown in combat configuration as pieces of history, reminding us of the great days of this extraordinary aircraft. (Norm Taylor)

136. As long as there is fuel to fly, it seems that a Flying Fortress will be in the air. This is the EAA Museum Foundation's B-17G, being chased by a Zero replica, during the annual convention at Oshkosh: it is duplicating a scene from *Tora! Tora! Tora!* (although with only one main wheel down a touch-and-go is all that is attempted here). (Eric Lundahl)